# SOLOS FOR THE SANCTUARY
# WORSHIP
## 9 PIANO SOLOS FOR THE CHURCH PIANIST

Arranged by Glenda Austin

ISBN 978-1-4768-1274-8

WILLIS MUSIC

EXCLUSIVELY DISTRIBUTED BY

## Hal•LEONARD®

Visit Hal Leonard Online at
**www.halleonard.com**

World headquarters, contact:
**Hal Leonard**
7777 West Bluemound Road
Milwaukee, WI 53213
Email: info@halleonard.com

In Europe, contact:
**Hal Leonard Europe Limited**
1 Red Place
London, W1K 6PL
Email: info@halleonardeurope.com

In Australia, contact:
**Hal Leonard Australia Pty. Ltd.**
4 Lentara Court
Cheltenham, Victoria, 3192 Australia
Email: info@halleonard.com.au

# PREFACE

I am excited about the latest addition to the *Solos for the Sanctuary* series: contemporary worship songs. If your church is anything like mine (and I'm guessing it is), you have had to adjust and adapt to different kinds of services. Somewhere along the way, I'm sure you've encountered one with a "blended" style of music. Initially, it was a little difficult to incorporate this music on the piano, but now there is a wealth of excellent arrangements available to church musicians. This book is my contribution.

Included from this contemporary genre are songs that I truly love. All have been carefully and thoughtfully chosen because I believe each and every one has real staying power. Just like many of our beloved hymns, these particular songs will stand the test of time and may become the standard "hymns" of tomorrow. Pianistically, I did my best to arrange these fairly predictable songs in a way that is a little more creative and unexpected, yet still pleasing to the ear. Please feel free to take liberties with tempo and dynamics and customize it to fit your mood. I seldom play anything the same way twice!

But most important:

> "Sing and make music to the Lord with your hearts."
>
> (Ephesians 5:19b, GW)

All the best,

*Glenda Austin*

# CONTENTS

# Above All

Words and Music by
Paul Baloche and Lenny LeBlanc
*Arranged by Glenda Austin*

**Moderately, with flexibility**

**Broadly**

**Tempo Primo**

# Change My Heart Oh God

Words and Music by
Eddie Espinosa
*Arranged by Glenda Austin*

**Moderately, with a gentle beat**

*With pedal*

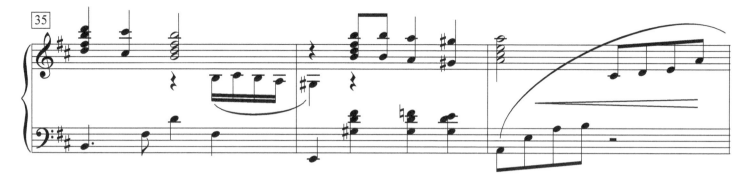

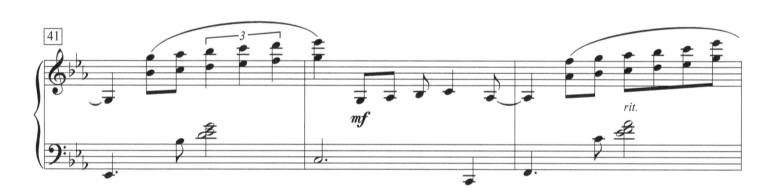

# Give Thanks
## (with "Now Thank We All Our God")

Words and Music by
Henry Smith
*Arranged by Glenda Austin*

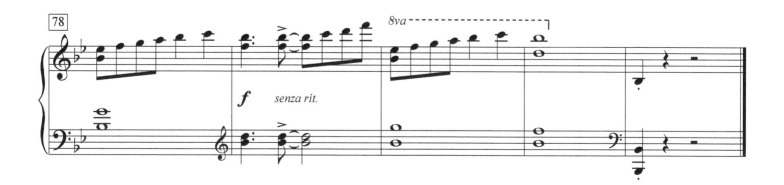

# Great Is the Lord

Words and Music by Michael W. Smith
and Deborah D. Smith
*Arranged by Glenda Austin*

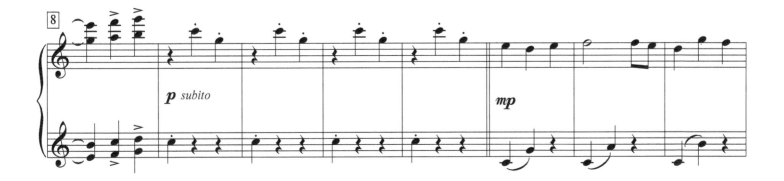

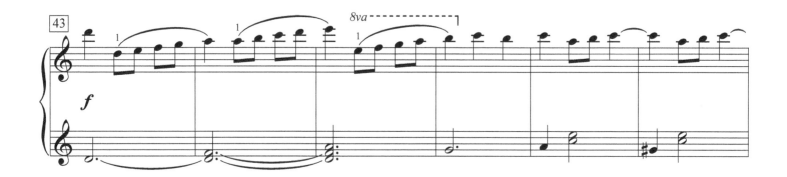

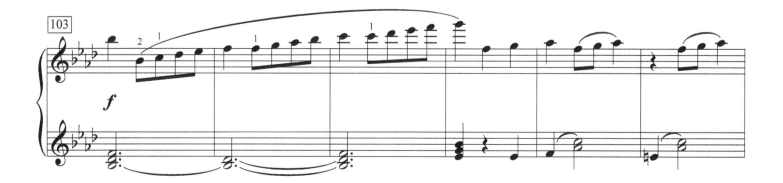

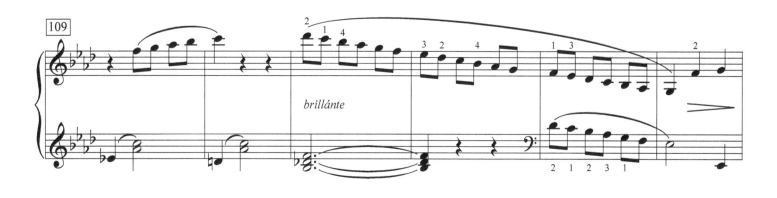

# How Great Is Our God

Words and Music by Chris Tomlin,
Jesse Reeves and Ed Cash
*Arranged by Glenda Austin*

**Warmly, with a steady beat**

*With pedal*

**Majestically**

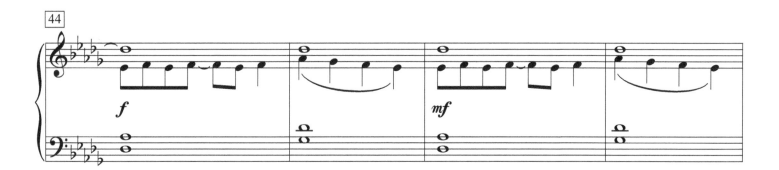

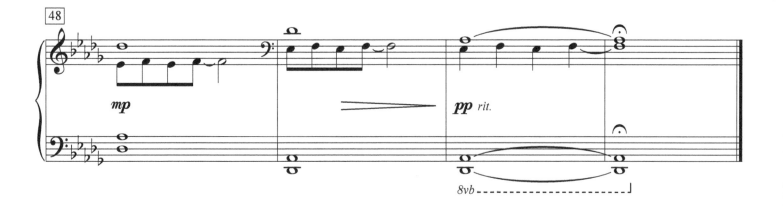

# How Majestic Is Your Name

Words and Music by
Michael W. Smith
*Arranged by Glenda Austin*

# There Is a Redeemer

Words and Music by
Melody Green
*Arranged by Glenda Austin*

**Gently, with expression**

# In Christ Alone

Words and Music by Keith Getty
and Stuart Townend
*Arranged by Glenda Austin*

28

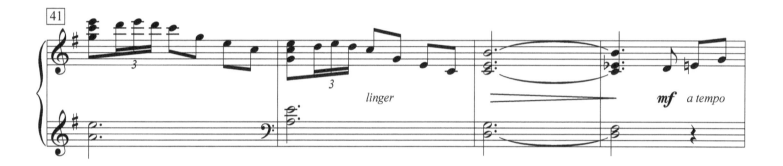

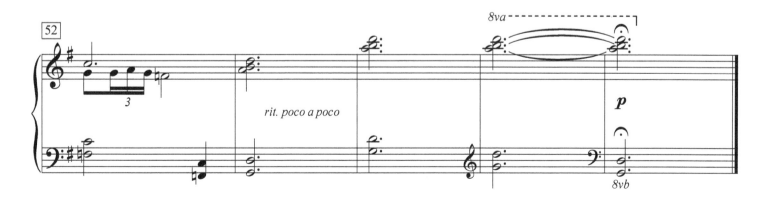

# You Are My All in All

By Dennis Jernigan
*Arranged by Glenda Austin*

**Reverently, simply and unhurried**

# ALSO AVAILABLE

**HL 396981 Solos for Sanctuary – SEASONS**
Church pianists will treasure this beautiful collection
featuring over 20 piano solos for the church year.